The Music in the Hallway

Written by
Tamara Shirece Jackson

As told to
Julie Ward-Weathington

Illustrated by
Darlene Shropshire

The Music in the Hallway

Written by Tamara Shirece Jackson
As told to Julie Ward-Weathington
Illustrated by Darlene Shropshire

The Music in the Hallway

My name is Takara and I'm a Treasure.
That's what my name means, "special treasure,"
but my auntie calls me, "Powderpuff."

Auntie told me about the music in the hallway.
My auntie was very sick and went into the hospital.

Auntie was in the hospital for a very long time.
They said I was too little to come in and see her, so we talked
on the phone. I could hear strange music in the background.

This kind of music is not made with trumpets, clarinets, or flutes, not drums, pianos or toot toots.

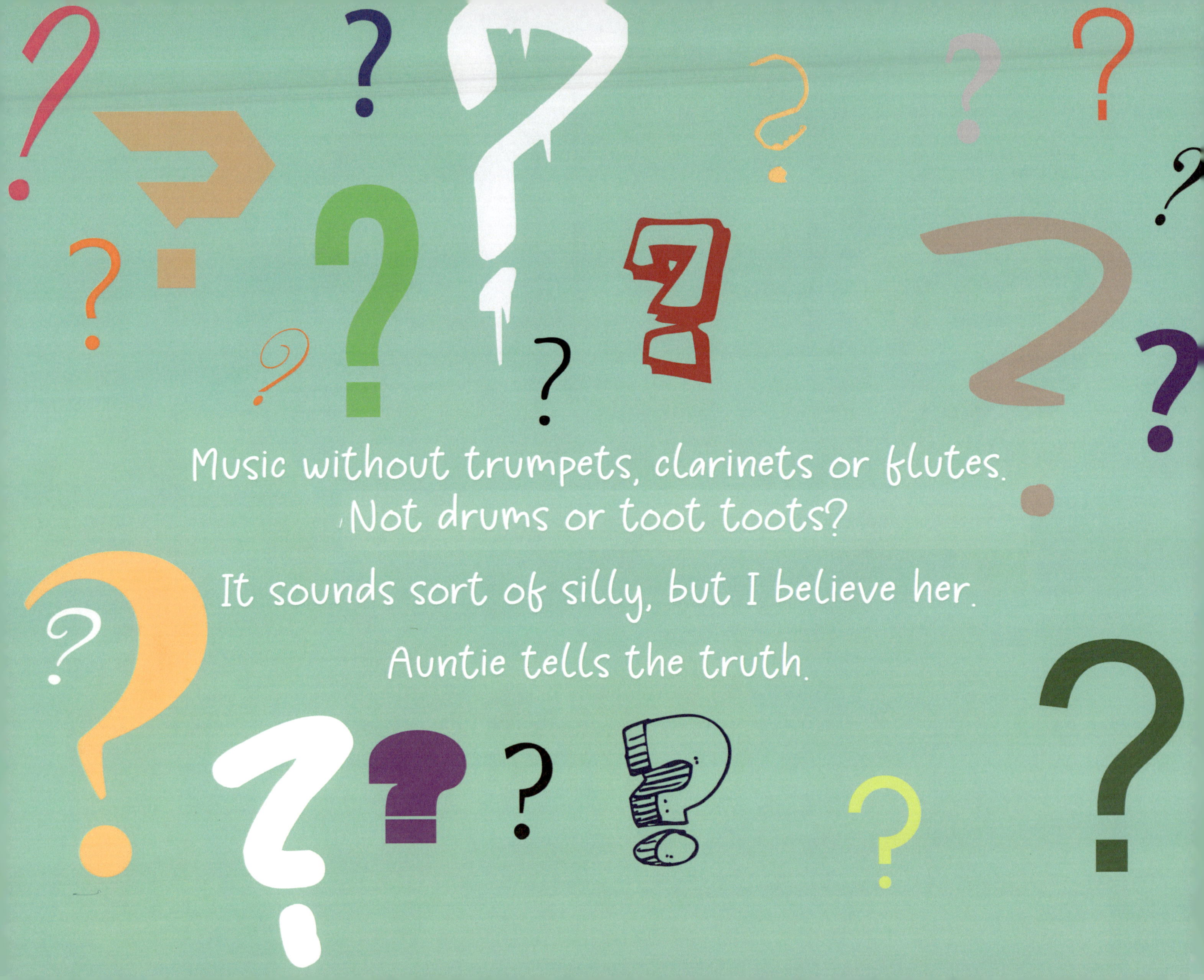

Music without trumpets, clarinets or flutes.
Not drums or toot toots?
It sounds sort of silly, but I believe her.
Auntie tells the truth.

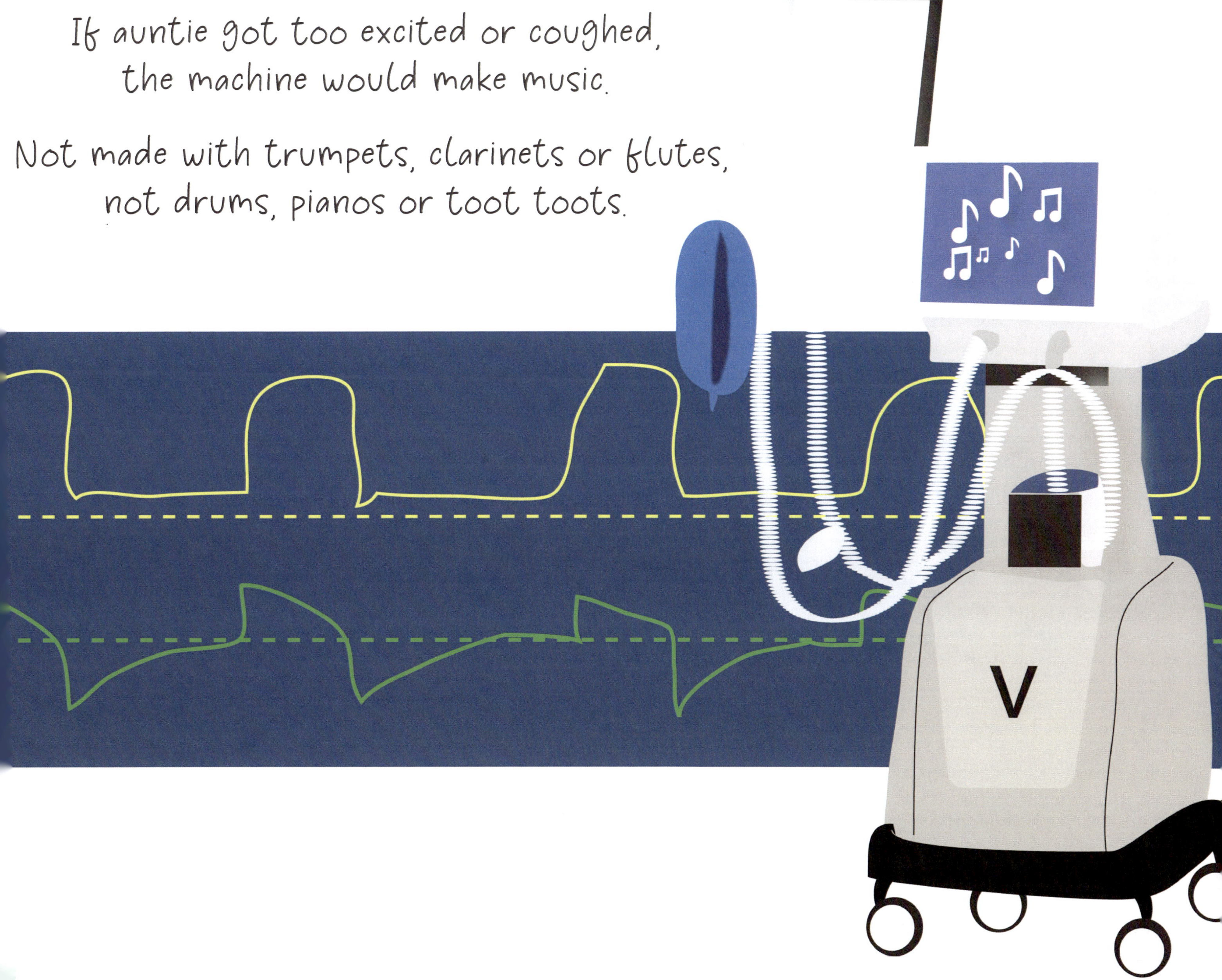

If auntie got too excited or coughed,
the machine would make music.

Not made with trumpets, clarinets or flutes,
not drums, pianos or toot toots.

Sometimes the music is on beat,
others would not make you tap your feet.

All you have to do is breathe. Sounds easy, huh?
Auntie could not breathe so easy these days.

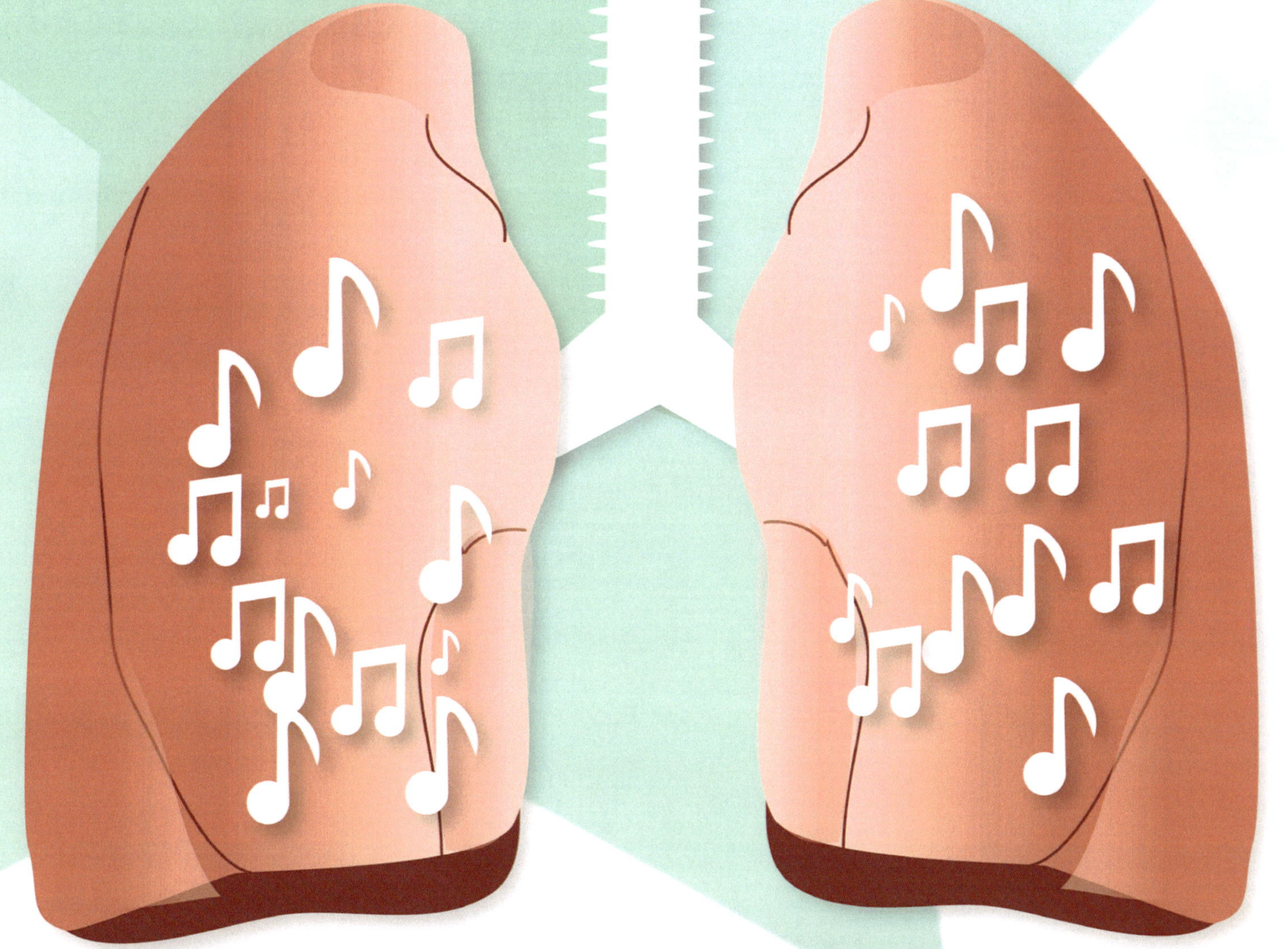

Auntie breathed through her neck where necklaces hang.
Have you ever tried to breathe through your throat?
Not so easy, huh?

My auntie said, "You almost forget that you have a nose."
I touched mine to be sure it was still there.

I couldn't wait for Auntie to get away from the music.
Not the music made with trumpets, clarinets or flutes,
not drums, pianos or toot toots.

This was hallway music.

he hallway music didn't sound so great.
missed Auntie, but I knew I had to wait.

Before I knew it she was home,
but it felt like she was gone too long.

Now we can make our own music.
Music with trumpets, clarinets and flutes,
drums, pianos and toot toots.